Read, Sing, and Learn Mini-Books:
FAMOUS AMERICANS

20 Reproducible Books With Mini-Bios, Fun Facts, Activities— and Super Songs Set to Familiar Tunes

by Rose Marie Crocco and Agnes Dunn

NEW YORK • TORONTO • LONDON • AUCKLAND • SYDNEY
MEXICO CITY • NEW DELHI • HONG KONG • BUENOS AIRES

*For our husbands,
Alan Dunn
and
Tony Crocco*

Acknowledgements

Many thanks to all of the educators in Stafford County, Virginia
who offered suggestions for activities or sang our songs with their students.
We also wish to thank Kama Einhorn for believing in us and making it possible
for us to share our mini-books with other educators.

Scholastic Inc. grants teachers permission to photocopy the pages from this book for classroom use. No other part of this publication may be reproduced in whole or in part, or stored in a retrieval system, or transmitted in any form or by any means, electronic, mechanical, photocopying, recording, or otherwise, without written permission of the publisher. For information regarding permission, write to Scholastic Inc., 557 Broadway, New York, NY 10012.

Cover design by Jim Sarfati
Cover and interior art by Alan Eitzen
Design by Solutions by Design, Inc.
Historical Consultant: Paul Ringel, Ph.D.

ISBN: 0-439-37665-3

Copyright 2002 by Rose Marie Crocco and Agnes Dunn.
All rights reserved. Printed in the U.S.A.

4 5 6 7 8 9 10   40   08 07 06

Contents

Welcome! 4

Cesar Chavez 5

Amelia Earhart 9

Thomas Alva Edison 13

Helen Keller 17

Meriwether Lewis and William Clark 21

Thurgood Marshall 25

Sally Ride 29

Jackie Robinson 33

Franklin Delano Roosevelt 37

Sacagawea 41

Daniel Boone 45

Paul Revere 49

Rosa Parks 53

Harriet Tubman 57

Susan B. Anthony 61

Abraham Lincoln 65

George Washington Carver 69

Martin Luther King, Jr. 73

George Washington 77

Welcome!

We began to collaborate on the activities and songs in this book when our state of Virginia implemented the Standards of Learning Assessment program, which identified the challenges facing educators in the area of social studies.

Very young children in particular have difficulty retaining facts and abstract concepts over time. We have found that reinforcing classroom content with reading and writing activities deepens understanding. Incorporating information into songs set to familiar tunes helps children recall facts—and, of course, is lots of fun! So we were pleased when Scholastic asked us to share our suggestions with other teachers.

For some historical figures, you'll be providing a review. For others, you'll help create much needed background knowledge to build a foundation for learning more in future grades. But, most of all, your children will learn difficult subject matter in a developmentally appropriate way.

And, remember, **sing out loud!**

—Rose Marie Crocco and Agnes Dunn

We welcome comments and suggestions from those who use our mini-books. We enjoyed writing them and we hope you and your students enjoy using them. You can contact us by e-mail at:
adunn@fls.infi.net
crocco@adelphia.net

This Book Provides

☆ Mini-biographies of twenty important figures in American history.

☆ A variety of reading, vocabulary and writing activities to provide meaningful learning experiences.

☆ Songs set to familiar children's tunes, to reinforce difficult-to-remember social studies content.

Making the Mini-Books

To construct the books, remove the pages carefully along the perforated edge. Make two-sided copies of each page for each child. Collate the pages of the book in number order. Carefully align all edges, fold along the gray line, and staple.

Using the Mini-Books

Sensory experiences increase children's comprehension and retention. Since young children do not have the skills (or patience!) to write notes to aid memory, our songs embed key facts in tunes, making information easier to retain.

Once you've made the mini-books, you might:

☆ Use the books to introduce a famous American, or use as reinforcement for subject matter you've already covered.

☆ Walk children through each page of the mini-book and complete them as a group. Older students might be able to work independently.

☆ Have children work in pairs to complete the mini-books, then have one child read the biography out loud.

☆ Have children color the mini-books.

☆ Invite children to bring them home and share with their families.

☆ Copy the songs onto chart paper.

☆ Sing the songs whenever you have a few minutes to spare!

Make Your Own!

Invite children to create their own mini-books about any famous American. They can use the format of the mini-book in this book for reference.

Cesar Chavez
1927–1993
Californian With a Cause

Cesar Chavez attended more than thirty schools before the eighth grade. What do you think it would be like to change schools that often?

_____
_____
_____
_____
_____
_____
_____
_____

Cesar Chavez was born in Yuma, Arizona in 1927. His family owned a farm and worked the land. During the years of the Great Depression, many farmers lost their crops and could not afford to keep their farms. When this happened to the Chavez family, they, like many other families, moved to California to look for work.

The family became migrant farm workers, moving from place to place to pick fruits and vegetables as they ripened. Because the family moved to harvest crops, Cesar Chavez changed schools more than thirty times. The family was so poor that Cesar often had to help with the picking and not go to school. After eighth grade, Cesar Chavez left school to take care of his parents.

Cesar Chavez was a farm worker all his life and, like other farm workers, toiled long hours for little pay. Many farm workers were made very ill by the dangerous chemicals used on the crops. There was no money for, and no one to protect, the many workers who were too sick or too old to work.

Cesar Chavez became determined to change these terrible conditions. He began by helping the Community Service Organization (C.S.O.).

CESAR CHAVEZ

(sing to the tune of "Ten Little Indians")

Cesar Chavez, migrant worker,
Helped set up a labor union,
Led a boycott, grapes and lettuce,
Fought for workers' rights.

Cesar Chavez, Mexican-American,
Led a workers' voting drive,
Boycotts, strikes, and peaceful marches,
Fought for workers' rights.

Many migrant workers were not American citizens, so were not allowed to vote. The C.S.O. helped workers to become citizens and gain a voice in government. To further their work, Cesar Chavez took classes at night and became a good speaker. In 1962, he helped begin the National Farm Workers Association.

Cesar Chavez led a boycott of California grapes and lettuce. He asked people not to buy lettuce or grapes until the workers who picked the produce were better treated. Many people in many parts of the world stopped buying these products. As fewer people bought lettuce and grapes, companies lost money and so began to listen to the workers' demands.

Cesar Chavez believed in peaceful protests. He organized boycotts, made speeches, and led marches. To make changes he felt were especially important, he went on hunger strikes, refusing to eat until certain practices were changed.

His brave work helped improve the lives of farm workers and made many agricultural practices safer for us all.

Cesar Chavez led peaceful protests to gain rights for migrant workers. Create a sign that might have been held up at a National Farm Workers Association (NFWA) meeting.

Did You Know...

☆ Cesar Chavez's family was so poor he did not always have shoes to wear. He walked barefoot to school.

☆ His family picked fruits and vegetables all year long: lettuce and peas in the winter, cherries and beans in the spring, grapes and corn in the summer, and cotton in the fall.

☆ Before farm workers worked to gain rights, farm owners could fire a worker for no reason!

☆ Cesar Chavez walked 250 miles from his home to Sacramento, the capital of California, to bring attention to the needs of farm workers.

Cesar Chavez and his family picked fruits and vegetables during each season of the year. They moved from farm to farm harvesting the ripe food. Draw a picture of the fruits and vegetables he picked in each season.

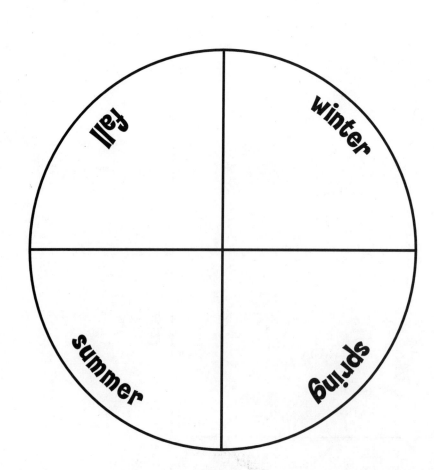

Amelia Earhart
1897–1937
First Lady of the Skies

HISTORY MYSTERY

What do you think happened to Amelia Earhart's plane?

_____
_____
_____
_____

Amelia Mary Earhart was born in Atchison, Kansas in 1897. She and her family lived with her grandparents for most of her childhood. Her grandparents were very wealthy and she attended private schools. During the First World War, she trained as a nurse's aid. She served as a nurse until the end of the war.

Soon after the war ended, her father took her for her first flight in an airplane. Later, she enjoyed flying so much she began taking flying lessons and bought her own plane, "The Canary." She became a social worker and saved money for building her own landing strip for her plane.

Amelia Earhart liked to try things that many other men and women would be afraid to do. In 1928, she was the first woman to travel over the Atlantic Ocean in an airplane. Airplanes had only been invented a few years before, and few people went on long flights. This flight took 20 hours and 40 minutes. Amelia Earhart became famous

Did You Know...

☆ When Amelia Earhart was little, her nickname was Millie.

☆ The first time she saw an airplane, she was 10. She thought it looked like it was made of rusty wire and wood. She did not think it was very interesting!

☆ She drove her bright yellow car from California to Boston!

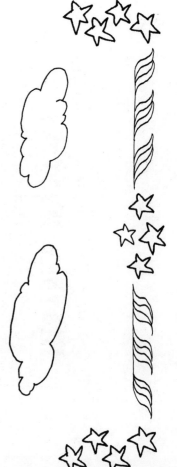

for this daring feat.

To encourage more women to learn to fly, she organized a cross-country race for airplanes piloted by women. She called it the Powder-Puff Derby. Ninety-nine women took part in the race. These independent women formed a now-famous group called the Ninety-Nines.

Amelia Earhart continued to have adventures. She was the first person to fly over both the Atlantic Ocean and the Pacific Ocean, and flew faster than any other woman. She piloted a plane from Hawaii to the United States mainland.

In 1937, Amelia Earhart took on her most daring adventure yet. She decided to fly around the world. She set off on her journey and flew 22,000 miles. Suddenly, over the ocean her plane disappeared. Amelia Earhart and her plane have never been found, but she is remembered as a brave adventurer.

During her trip around the world, Amelia Earhart flew to five continents. Can you name them?

1. _____
2. _____
3. _____
4. _____
5. _____

AMELIA EARHART

(sing to the tune of "Twinkle, Twinkle")

Amelia Earhart flew the skies
Breaking records way up high.
Cross Atlantic's ocean blue
Flew across Pacific, too.
Around the world was her last flight,
When her plane dropped out of sight.

If you could fly anywhere in an airplane, where would you go?

_____
_____
_____

Why? _____
_____
_____
_____
_____

Thomas Alva Edison
1847–1931

The Wizard of Menlo Park

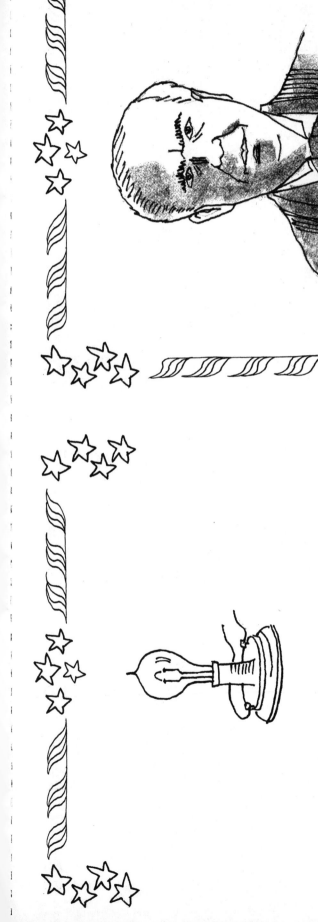

1

Thomas Edison's most famous saying was: "Genius is one percent inspiration and ninety-nine percent perspiration."

What do you think he meant?

_____
_____
_____
_____
_____

8

Thomas Alva Edison was born in Ohio in 1847. As a boy, he liked to experiment and make things. He set up a chemistry lab in his house. When he was fifteen years old, he built a printing press, then wrote and printed his own newspaper. A few years later, he invented his first machine. The machine was a vote counter to be used in elections.

One day, when he was at work, an important machine that recorded stock prices broke down. Rather than fix the machine, Thomas Edison designed a better one. He was paid $40.00 for his invention. In those days, this was a fortune.

Thomas Edison used this money to set up a lab in Menlo Park, New Jersey. There, many talented people worked with him to create inventions from his ideas. This was the first laboratory for inventions in the United States. Thomas Edison had so many ideas that he knew his lab would produce many new things.

THOMAS ALVA EDISON

(sing to the tune of "Ten Little Indians")

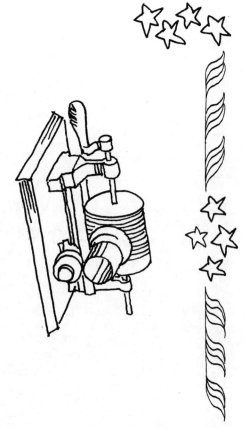

Edison was an inventor
Of many useful tools and appliances
Some he improved on the works of others
The Wizard of Menlo Park

A voting machine, his first invention
Electric light bulb, most important
Phonograph, most original
The Wizard of Menlo Park

He promised that the lab would produce a simple invention every ten days and an important invention every six months. Many people thought he was bragging, but he was not. He came up with so many inventions, he was nicknamed the "Wizard of Menlo Park." Many of Thomas Edison's inventions are still used today. The one that we probably use the most often is the light bulb.

Fill in the words to describe Thomas Edison and his inventions in the spaces below.

1. The first laboratory built to make inventions was in _____.

2. Thomas Edison's favorite invention was the _____.

3. His first invention was a machine that counts _____.

4. The invention we use every day is the _____ bulb.

5. Thomas Edison earned $40 for a machine that records _____ prices.

1. _ _ _ _
2. _ _ _ _ _
3. _ _ _ _
4. _ _ _ _
5. _ _ _ _ _

Now write the letters in the boxes to show what his work led to!

$\overline{1}\ \overline{2}\ \overline{3}\ \overline{4}\ \overline{5}$
          e

Read, Sing, and Learn Mini-Books: Famous Americans Scholastic Professional Books

Did You Know...

☆ Thomas Edison was partially deaf. He wrote in his diary, "I haven't heard a bird sing since I was 12 years old."

☆ Some of his experiments did not work, like the time he tried to separate iron ore from dirt and rocks.

☆ The first words Edison recorded on his phonograph were, "Mary had a little lamb."

☆ During World War I, Thomas Edison made a low-priced phonograph. Many Army units bought them to let the soldiers take their music overseas.

THE PHONOGRAPH

The phonograph was Thomas Edison's favorite invention. He hoped people would find many ways to use his invention. He even suggested several possible uses:

☐ Music boxes
☐ Taking dictation in offices
☐ Clocks that say the time out loud
☐ Talking books for blind people
☐ Toys that make noise
☐ Recording the voices of family and friends

Put a check in the box beside each of Edison's suggestions that are in use today. Can you think of any other ways we use recorded sound?

_____
_____

Helen Keller

1880–1968

A Voice for Those Less Fortunate

1

PROBLEM & SOLUTION

Helen Keller was a good problem solver. Describe a problem you have and a possible solution.

_____
_____
_____
_____
_____
_____
_____

8

Helen Keller was born in 1880. When she was born, she could see and hear. As babies do, she babbled and learned to say her first words. Then, when she was two years old, she came down with a serious illness. This disease left her unable to see or to hear. If you close your eyes and cover your ears, you can imagine how lonely and scared she must have been. The only way for her to know about the world around her was through her sense of touch. She could not tell if anyone was near her unless they were touching her. Because she could not hear, she stopped learning to talk. Communicating was close to impossible. Sometimes, she could act out what she wanted. Often, she cried and screamed in frustration. Her family found these tantrums frightening and difficult to manage.

When Helen Keller was seven years old, a special teacher named Anne Sullivan came into her life. Anne Sullivan helped Helen to feel less lonely and afraid. As Helen learned to stay calmer, Anne Sullivan began teaching her a sign-language finger alphabet. She would touch Helen's palm in a different way for each letter of the alphabet. One day, she took Helen to the water pump. She

HELEN KELLER
(sing to the tune of "Clementine")

Helen Keller was a young girl
Couldn't hear or speak or see
But a teacher came to help her
Speak and read like you and me

Wrote the letters in her hand
with the Braille alphabet
Learned to speak by feeling rhythm
Spoke for those less fortunate

touched Helen's hand with the signs for W-A-T-E-R, then ran water onto her hand. She did this again and again. Suddenly Helen understood! The taps on her hand stood for real things. Helen ran around all day touching things and learning the signed names for them.

As she grew, Helen learned to sign whole sentences. Later, she learned to use a Braille typewriter. This was a machine that stamped different patterns of raised bumps for each letter of the alphabet. Blind people read Braille by feeling the bumps with their fingers.

Helen attended the Perkins School for the Blind and then Radcliffe College. While she was in college, Helen Keller wrote "The Story of My Life."

Helen Keller helped in the fight to give women the right to vote. She began groups to support people with physical challenges.

Helen Keller was the first blind-deaf person to become so well known. Her work took courage and helped everyone to know that those with physical challenges can lead rich lives, full of accomplishment.

THE BRAILLE ALPHABET

Use the Braille alphabet to write the letters in the blanks below.

.	:	·.	·:	·.	:.	::	·:	.·	
A	B	C	D	E	F	G	H	I	
:·	:	:.	::	:·	::.	::	·:	·:.	
J	K	L	M	N	O	P	Q	R	
.:	.:·	·:·	::	:·:	·::				
S	T	U	V	W	X	Y	Z		

How did Helen Keller read? She:

_____

_____

Did You Know...

★ Alexander Graham Bell was a friend of the Keller family. He told her parents to contact the Perkins School for the blind. That is how Anne Sullivan became Helen's teacher.

★ Anne Sullivan stayed Helen's friend and teacher until she died.

★ Helen could "listen" to a person by putting her fingers beside their nose, lips and on their throat.

★ Helen Keller gave speeches in 25 countries.

★ During World War Two, Helen Keller worked to help soldiers that had become blind during the war.

THE FIVE SENSES

Our senses are how we learn about the world around us. Our senses tell our brain that ice cream is sweet, a kitten is soft, our favorite music sounds pretty, dinner smells good, or our friend's hair is red. If we lose the use of one of our senses, the others get stronger. Draw a picture of the body part used for each sense.

| seeing | hearing | touching |

| smelling | tasting |

Now put an X on the senses Helen could not use. Circle the sense Helen used most.

Meriwether Lewis
1774–1809

William Clark
1770–1838

Led a Voyage of Discovery

1

YOUR OWN JOURNAL

Lewis and Clark kept a journal on their trip. They made maps of the land they saw, and drew pictures of plants and animals.

Write and illustrate your own journal entry for yesterday. What did you do? Who did you see?

8

Meriwether Lewis was born in Virginia in 1774. William Clark was born in Virginia in 1770. Although Lewis and Clark did not know each other as children, there were similarities in their childhoods. Both grew up in Virginia, where they hunted and spent lots of time in the forest. Meriwether Lewis attended more school than did William Clark. Because his family was poor, William Clark spent much of his time hunting to help feed his family.

Both men served in the army where they met and became friends. William Clark stayed in the army only a short time. Meriwether Lewis stayed in the army for many years.

Meriwether Lewis became Secretary to President Thomas Jefferson. When the United States bought the Louisiana Territory from France, President Jefferson needed someone to explore and map this vast and largely unexplored part of the West. He wanted to find a route through the territory to the Pacific Ocean. President Jefferson asked his Secretary to undertake the trip.

Meriwether Lewis agreed to lead the expedition, and asked his friend William Clark to join him. William Clark was a good choice to help lead the expedition as he was good at drawing maps, navigating, and working with people.

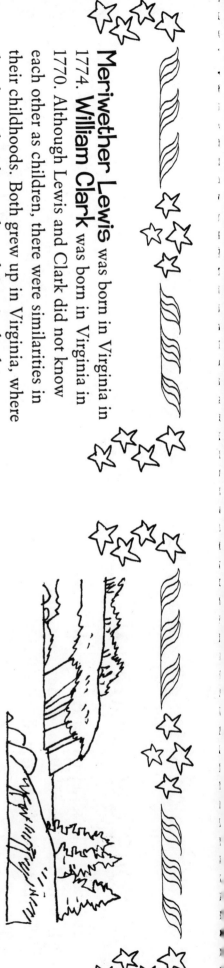

LEWIS AND CLARK

(sing to the tune of "Clementine")

Through the canyons, over mountains,
Down the rivers flowing free,
Clark and Lewis led a journey
From St. Louis to the sea.

Thomas Jefferson bought the area,
But he didn't have a clue
About the animals, plants and people
And he needed good maps, too.

They kept a journal, recorded weather,
Met with natives on the way.
8,000 miles they did travel,
Famous journey to this day.

The expedition set off in 1804 with 29 people, three boats, and many supplies. President Jefferson had medals made up to give to Native American leaders the party might meet along the way. The medals, which showed two people shaking hands, were meant to show the Native Americans that the group came in peace.

As they traveled along the Missouri River and through the Great Plains, William Clark mapped their journey. Meriwether Lewis kept a journal with drawings of the Native American tribes they met. He made many drawings of the animals and plants they saw.

Along their way, they met a Native American woman named Sacagewea. She and her family, including her very young baby, traveled with them for much of the way. She helped them to find food and to communicate and trade with some of the Native Americans they met.

The explorers made their way over the Rocky Mountains and came to the ocean, at last. The expedition had been successful: they had found a route to the Pacific. By the time the explorers had re-traced their footsteps and returned to St. Louis, they had explored 8,000 miles in two years.

President Jefferson was very pleased at their success and their safe return. He made both Meriwether Lewis and William Clark governors of part of the territory they had explored.

LEWIS AND CLARK TIMELINE

Draw a line from each event to the correct place on the timeline.

☆ Sacagawea joins the journey.

☆ President Jefferson asks Lewis to explore Louisiana.

☆ Lewis becomes Thomas Jefferson's secretary.

☆ The travelers arrive back in St. Louis.

☆ Thomas Jefferson becomes President.

☆ President Jefferson purchases Louisiana from France.

1801 —

1802 —

1803 —

1804 —

1805 —

1806 —

Read, Sing, and Learn Mini-Books: Famous Americans Scholastic Professional Books

Did You Know...

☆ Meriwether Lewis gathered live animals to send back home. President Jefferson collected birds, so Lewis sent him a Magpie (a type of bird).

☆ Meriwether Lewis reached the Continental Divide (the top of the Rocky Mountains) on his 31st birthday.

☆ William Clark became friends with Sacagawea's son. He gave him the nickname "Pomp." Several years after the journey ended, Pomp went to live with William Clark and go to school.

☆ One of the men in the expedition was blind in one eye. One day, while hunting, he thought Lewis was an elk and shot him. Clark was good at first aid, and helped Lewis get well.

Lewis and Clark were good friends, but they were not very much alike. Maybe this is why they were a good team! Write the things that are alike for you and a friend in the center. Write the things that are different in each oval.

Me _____

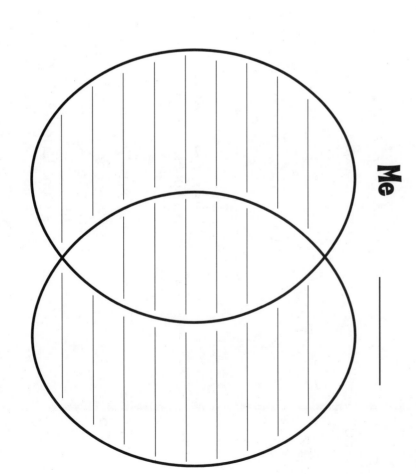

Thurgood Marshall

1908–1993

Mr. Civil Rights

Thurgood Marshall, in a speech at Dillard College, said, "It takes no courage to throw a rock."

What do you think he meant?

_____
_____
_____
_____
_____
_____
_____

Thurgood Marshall was born in Baltimore, Maryland in 1908. His mother taught in an African-American school, and his father was a waiter on a railroad dining car. Education was very important to his family, and Thurgood Marshall was a good student. At a time when few African-Americans went to college, he went to both Lincoln University and Howard University Law School. He did so well that he graduated from both Universities with honors.

Thurgood Marshall became a lawyer. He worked as head lawyer for the NAACP, a national group that works to secure and protect the rights of African-Americans.

At that time, in the part of the United States in which Thurgood Marshall lived, there were laws to keep African-Americans separate from other Americans in many public places. African-American children could not go to school with white children. In buses and some restaurants, African-Americans had to sit in an area away from whites. This practice was known as segregation. African-Americans were not allowed in many well-paying jobs, so they were often poor. As a lawyer, Thurgood Marshall worked to prove that

THURGOOD MARSHALL
(sing to the tune of "Ten Little Indians")

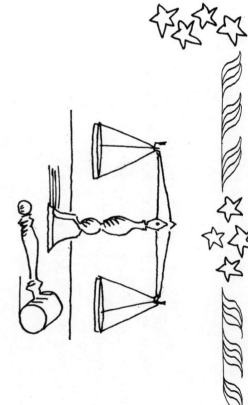

Thurgood Marshall fought for justice,
First Supreme Court African-American
Helped us all end segregation,
Mr. Civil Rights.

Thurgood Marshall, freedom fighter,
Lawyer, judge, Supreme Court Justice
Used the courts to change our country,
Mr. Civil Rights.

the laws enforcing segregation were not allowed by the rules of the United States Constitution.

A landmark case he argued is known as Brown versus the Board of Education. When their daughter was not allowed to attend a public school near their house, because it was a white-only school, the Browns sued the Board of Education in Topeka, Kansas. Thurgood Marshall argued the case before the United States Supreme Court. On May 17, 1954, the court decided it was illegal to segregate public schools.

Of the 32 cases he argued before the United States Supreme Court, Thurgood Marshall won 29. By winning these cases, he helped African-Americans access the rights that belong to all American citizens. These rights are called Civil Rights, so, for his work, Thurgood Marshall is known as "Mr. Civil Rights."

Later, Thurgood Marshall was named a federal judge. In 1967, he was appointed to the United States Supreme Court, becoming the first African-American Supreme Court Justice. He served for more than 20 years and continued to help restore and protect the civil rights of all Americans.

THE FIVE W'S

Pretend you are gathering information on Thurgood Marshall for a newspaper article. Fill in the blanks below.

Who _____

What (an important thing he did) _____

When (an important date and time) _____

Where (an important place in his life) _____

Why (the reason we learn about him today) _____

Did You Know...

☆ When he was young, Thurgood Marshall was sometimes naughty. He had to read the United States Constitution as punishment. He once said that by the time he graduated from high school, he had memorized the whole thing!

☆ His mother wanted him to become a dentist.

☆ After graduating from college, Thurgood Marshall applied to the University of Maryland Law School. However, they did not let African-American students attend.

☆ Thurgood Marshall and his family were very proud of their heritage. They traced their roots back to an African who lived in the 1800s.

Segregation

Definition: The practice of keeping people of different races or groups apart.

What is it like? (Characteristics)

- Unfair
-
-
-

Segregation

Example: African-Americans had to have separate stores.

Example:

Example:

Sally Ride

(born 1951)

Reaching for the Stars

NASA SEEKS FIRST STUDENT IN SPACE!

What if NASA advertised in a newspaper that they were looking for the first student astronaut? Explain why you think they should pick you (or a friend, if you don't want the job!).

_____
_____
_____
_____
_____
_____

Sally Ride was born on May 26, 1951 in Encino, California. As a young girl, she liked learning about science and using her telescope to look at the stars. When she was in high school, she was one of the best tennis players in the country. For a while, she played tennis full-time.

Sally Ride went to Stanford University. She studied English and Physics and earned four degrees.

One day, she saw a newspaper ad asking for scientists to apply to NASA to become space shuttle astronauts. She and 8000 other people applied for the job. Sally Ride was one of the 35 people chosen.

In 1983, Sally Ride flew into space aboard the space shuttle Challenger. She was the first American woman to go into space, and the youngest astronaut ever. On the flight, she worked the shuttle's robot arm and helped to do experiments.

SALLY RIDE

(sing to the tune of "Yankee Doodle")

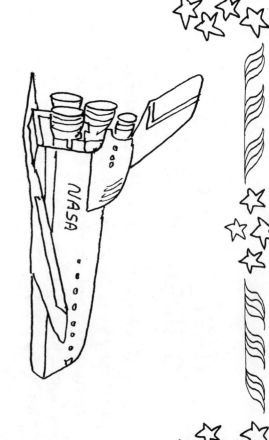

Sally Ride went up in space,
First female astronaut,
Rode the shuttle Challenger,
And liked it quite a lot.

Sally Ride, scientist,
Released a satellite,
Helped take off and land the flight,
She flew brave through the night.

A year later, Sally Ride again flew into space aboard the Challenger. On this mission, she used the robot arm to release a satellite into orbit.

Today, Sally Ride teaches at the University of California. She writes children's books. Her first book, *To Space and Back*, is the story of her space flight. She encourages young women to study science and think about going into space. She hopes they will reach for the stars!

SPACE WORDS

Draw lines to connect the words to their definitions.

galaxy   National Aeronautics and Space Administration

NASA   A specific path followed by a planet

orbit   A cluster of stars, dust and gas

Did You Know...

☆ Sally Ride's first trip into space lasted six days. Her second was eight days long.

☆ When you sleep in space, all of your muscles relax. Your arms and legs float up in front of you!

☆ On their first trip into space, the Challenger crew took along a jar of peanut butter, bread, and M&Ms.

☆ Sally Ride was a flight engineer on the space shuttle. She helped with take-off and re-entry (landing).

☆ She served on the committee that investigated the Challenger accident.

EARTH FROM SPACE

Draw what you think the Earth would look like from space.

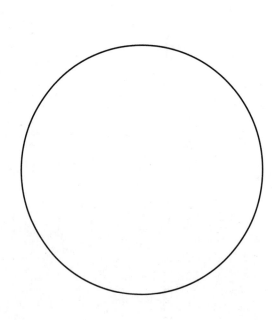

Describe what you drew.

_____
_____
_____
_____

Jackie Robinson

1919–1972

Opened the Bases to All of the Races

1

It was very hard for Jackie Robinson to be the first African-American player in Major League Baseball. Why do you think he wanted to do it anyway?

_____

_____

_____

_____

_____

8

Jackie Robinson was born in Cairo, Georgia in 1919. He grew up poor, and his parents were sharecroppers. They farmed land that they rented, and had to give the landowner part of each harvest as rent. Jackie Robinson's parents encouraged him to get a good education.

After attending junior college, Jackie Robinson went to the University of California at Los Angeles. There, he won many sports awards.

After college, Jackie Robinson joined the Army. At that time, professional sports had all-white teams, so he could not make a living playing sports.

Jackie Robinson was upset at the treatment of African-Americans in the Army and in daily life. One day, he refused to give up his seat on an Army bus for a white soldier. (This was 1944, ten years before Rosa Parks did the same thing on a public bus and became famous.) He was arrested. Although he was cleared of the charges, Jackie Robinson decided to leave the Army.

JACKIE ROBINSON

(sing to the tune of "Take Me Out to the Ballgame")

Jackie Robinson played ball.
Jackie played in New York.
Not all the players were glad he came.
Not many fans at his very first game.
But, it's root, root, root for the Dodgers.
And, Jackie proved he could play.
He opened the bases to all of the races,
A new ball game.

He began playing professional baseball with the African-American League. A year later, he was signed to the Brooklyn Dodgers. Now, he was the first African-American on a Major League team. Branch Rickey, the Dodgers manager, took a big chance in signing him. He warned Jackie Robinson that racist teammates and fans would not like the idea of African-American and white players on a team together.

At first, it was difficult for Jackie Robinson, but he helped people to give up their prejudices. He was a great player on a great team. In the ten years that Jackie Robinson played for the Dodgers, the team won six National League titles and a World Series.

When Jackie Robinson retired from baseball, he became a successful businessman. He helped other African-Americans to begin businesses, and he became a Special Assistant to the Governor of New York. In 1962, Jackie Robinson became the first African-American to be inducted into the Baseball Hall of Fame.

On Jackie Robinson's tombstone is a famous saying of his: "A life is not important except in the impact it has on other lives."

BASEBALL CARDS

Major League players have baseball cards that tell all about them. Create an all-about-me card in the rectangle below.

JACKIE ROBINSON

Name: _____

Nickname: _____

Hometown: _____

Birth date: _____

Hobbies: _____
_____
_____
_____

Did You Know...

☆ Jackie Robinson earned varsity letters for four sports in college: football, basketball, baseball and track. No other player at UCLA had ever done this!

☆ Baseball was actually not his best sport, but it was the only sport African-Americans could play professionally at that time.

☆ In his first major league game with the Dodgers, he did not have a hit. He scored the winning run on an error.

☆ Jackie Robinson won the first Rookie of the Year award. Today, it is called the Jackie Robinson award.

THE NATIONAL LEAGUE

Jackie Robinson played in the National League. Today, the National League has 16 teams. Circle their names in the puzzle below.

P	I	R	A	T	E	S	G	E	B	Z	M	A	P
H	Q	L	T	Y	V	B	I	X	R	M	A	D	
I	A	S	T	R	O	S	A	P	A	V	R	R	
L	G	U	I	S	E	Y	N	O	V	R	R		
L	R	E	D	S	M	E	T	S	E	L	E		
I	D	O	D	G	E	R	S	K	S	I	S		
E	R	O	C	K	I	E	S	B	U	N	T		
S	C	A	R	D	I	N	A	L	S	S	Q		
D	I	A	M	O	N	D	B	A	C	K	S		
B	R	E	W	E	R	S	X	C	U	B	S		

Astros Cubs Giants Phillies
Braves Diamondbacks Marlins Pirates
Brewers Dodgers Mets Reds
Cardinals Expos Padres Rockies

Franklin Delano Roosevelt

1882–1945

Our Longest Leader

Dear Mr. President

☆☆☆☆☆☆
☆☆☆☆☆☆

During the Great Depression, many people could not find jobs. Pretend that your mom or dad has just found a job for the first time in two years! Write President Roosevelt and tell him how happy your family is with the New Deal.

_____
_____
_____
_____
_____

Franklin Delano Roosevelt

Franklin Delano Roosevelt was born in Hyde Park, New York, in 1882. He grew up in a very wealthy family. His parents taught him that it was important to help those who were not well off.

In 1921, he and his wife, Eleanor, went to the ocean for a vacation. He swam and hiked, but later in the day, his legs felt strange. Two days later, he could not feel his legs at all. Franklin Roosevelt had caught a disease called polio that left him unable to walk. This was before doctors discovered a vaccine to protect people from polio.

Franklin Delano Roosevelt had to be in a wheelchair but kept right on going, doing many important things. He served two terms as Governor of New York, and in 1932 became president of the United States. America called him by his initials, FDR.

FDR became president during a difficult time called the Great Depression. Many Americans had lost their life savings and their jobs. Franklin Delano Roosevelt promised to

FRANKLIN ROOSEVELT
(sing to the tune of "Clementine")

Franklin Roosevelt was the president
So much longer than the rest
But then, the Great Depression
It put Franklin to the test.

Many agencies, lots of programs
To get jobs for all the poor.
The New Deal helped the nation
No Depression, anymore.

World War II came; FDR led.
Led our nation in the war.
Joined the Allies in the fighting
And then peace, it came once more.

end the Great Depression. He said, "The only thing we have to fear is fear itself." He and his close advisors, called his Cabinet, devised a plan to bring prosperity back to the country. This was called the New Deal. Part of this plan helped people who lost their jobs. Another part created new jobs for people who needed them.

FDR was near the end of his second term as President when the Second World War began in Europe. He thought that the country might be better off continuing with the same leader at this difficult time, so he ran for a third term. He was the first American President elected to a third term. In fact, he was even elected to a fourth term, but he died shortly afterward. Americans were very sad to lose this man who had led the country for over 12 years.

CREATE A STAMP

The United States Postal Service makes stamps to honor famous Americans like FDR. Use the boxes below to create stamps for people you feel are special, even if they are not as famous as FDR.

Did You Know...

★ FDR came from a very important family. He was related to eleven United States presidents! His wife's mother traced her family to thirteen relatives that came to America with the Pilgrims.

★ During the first 100 days of FDR's presidency, Congress passed more laws than they had ever passed before.

★ Thousands of pictures were taken of FDR during his presidency, but very few show him in his wheelchair.

★ Franklin Roosevelt is one of only four presidents to have a memorial on the Mall in Washington, D.C.

THE NEW DEAL

Fill in the blanks with words from the box to complete the paragraph.

| work | schools | Great Depression |
| bridges | FDR | hired |

_____ had a plan to end the _____. He wanted to put Americans back to _____. He _____ them to build _____, hospitals and airports. Other workers created new parks. These government jobs helped the economy.

Sacagawea

1788–1812

A Symbol of Peace

✭✭✭✭✭✭ Pack Your Bag! ✭✭✭✭✭✭

Pretend you are going along with Sacagawea and her family on the Lewis and Clark journey. Write five things you would like to pack and take along. (Remember that the travelers walked and paddled canoes the entire way, so you have to carry anything you bring!)

_____
_____
_____
_____
_____

Sacagawea born in Idaho in 1788. Her father was a Shoshone chief. When she was twelve years old, Sacagawea was kidnapped to another village. She lived with the Hidatsa until her marriage to Toussaint Charbonneau, a French Canadian trader.

During the winter of 1804-1805, an expedition of European-Americans came into the Mandan village in which Sacagawea and Toussaint Charbonneau were living. This was the famous expedition led by Lewis and Clark to explore the Louisiana Territory. Lewis and Clark decided to stay with the Mandan until winter had passed. Shortly after their arrival, Sacagawea had a son, whom she named Jean-Baptiste.

In the spring, Lewis and Clark asked Sacagawea and her family to join the expedition. Sacagawea could help the travelers since she spoke several Native American languages. Sacagawea wanted to see the ocean, so she agreed to join them, carrying the infant Jean-Baptiste on her back.

Sacagawea guided the party through the Shoshone lands she had known as a girl. She helped the party survive by finding plants that were good to eat. In one of the Shoshone groups

SACAGAWEA
(sing to the tune of "On Top of Old Smokey")

Oh, Sacagawea
Shoshone by birth
Lived with the Mandans
She studied their words

Lewis and Clark asked
Her whole family
"Let's journey cross country
And on to the sea."

She helped them buy horses
Translate and survive
They traded and made maps
and returned alive

that they met as they crossed the Rocky Mountains, Sacagawea met her brother. He was the new chief of the Shoshone. Sacagawea helped Lewis and Clark barter with him, trading for goods that they needed to complete the trip.

Sacagawea was a symbol of peace to the Native Americans. Women do not travel with Native American war parties, so those they met knew right away that the explorers did not intend to start a war.

The expedition successfully reached the Pacific Ocean, and then retraced their journey back home. Lewis and Clark said goodbye to Sacagawea and her family in the Mandan village in which they had met.

WORD SEARCH

Find the following words in the puzzle below. Circle each word.

Sacagawea journey
Clark horses
Lewis Pacific
Shoshone

S	H	O	S	H	O	N	E
A	A	I	J	O	B	C	K
C	C	L	A	R	K	M	L
A	H	F	G	S	D	E	N
G	R	Q	L	E	W	I	S
A	S	U	V	S	P	O	T
W	P	A	C	I	F	I	C
E	J	O	U	R	N	E	Y
A	G	R	S	E	P	N	S

Did You Know...

☆ At birth, Sacagawea's name was Boinaiv, which means "grass maiden."

☆ Translating for Lewis and Clark was a long process. Sacagawea would translate the words to Hidatsa, a native language her husband spoke. He translated them into French, which one of the men in the traveling party spoke. Then that man translated them into English.

☆ There is a lot of debate over when Sacagawea died. One story says she returned to her people and lived to be 100. Most historians think she died in 1812.

SACAGAWEA DOLLAR

In 2000, the United States honored Sacagawea with her own coin. Have you ever seen a Sacagawea dollar? It shows her carrying her son on the front, and a soaring American eagle on the back.

In the two circles below, design a coin to honor yourself. Draw your picture on one side. On the other, draw something special you do.

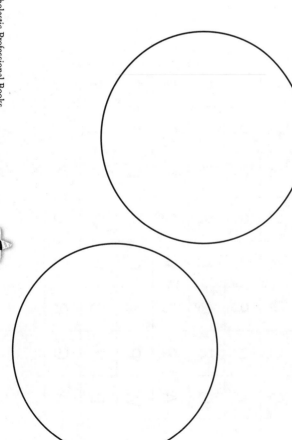

Daniel Boone

1734-1820

American Pioneer

Make a list of things you would take if you were going exploring.

_____
_____
_____
_____
_____
_____
_____

Daniel Boone was born in Reading, Pennsylvania in 1734. As a child, he loved to be outdoors and spent lots of time hunting and exploring. As he grew up, he learned more about the ways of outdoor life from his Native American friends.

One of Daniel Boone's first explorations was with a military expedition during the French and Indian War. Following this trip, he fell in love with and married Rebecca Bryan. Together they had ten children.

Daniel Boone had a friend, John Finley, who was a hunter and told exciting stories about exploring. Daniel Boone was inspired, and set out to the unexplored areas of Kentucky, Ohio, West Virginia, and Missouri. He led settlers to land that would be good for farming. Often this was dangerous because Native Americans did not want settlement on the lands where they lived.

DANIEL BOONE

(sing to the tune of "She'll Be Coming 'Round the Mountain")

He'll be traveling 'cross the country,
Daniel Boone
Westward Ho! across the country,
Daniel Boone
Hunting bears and squirrels, raccoons
The frontiersman, Daniel Boone
Brave explorer, pioneer, Daniel Boone

As more and more people settled in Kentucky, Daniel moved his family and other settlers West to Missouri. For the rest of his life, Daniel Boone continued to hunt and explore the Western Territories.

Today, Daniel Boone is remembered as an American legend and a true folk hero. He reminds us of the courage of the rugged pioneers who traveled the wild frontier.

Daniel Boone sent a postcard to his wife during his exploring days. What do you think he wrote to her?

Rebecca Bryan

Did You Know...

☆ Daniel Boone was born in a log cabin.

☆ He had very little schooling.

☆ He lived to be 85 years old.

☆ He is buried beside his wife, on a "high, far-seeing place" much like the land he explored and helped settle during his lifetime.

SIGHTS AND SOUNDS OF EXPLORING

Think about your five senses and describe what Daniel Boone may have experienced when he went exploring.

What did he see?
_____

What did he hear?
_____

What did he smell?
_____

What did he feel?
_____

What did he taste?
_____

Paul Revere
1735–1818
Freedom Rider

1

Draw yourself on Paul Revere's horse!

8

Paul Revere

Paul Revere was born in Boston, Massachusetts in 1735. When he was growing up, Boston was a busy seaport town. Paul Revere's father was a silversmith, and so when he was 13, Paul Revere left school and began learning smithing in his father's shop. As a young man, he joined the Sons of Liberty. They called themselves Patriots: patriotic Americans who wanted the colonies to be free from British rule.

Paul Revere became both a silversmith and goldsmith. He illustrated books and magazines and drew political cartoons. He also worked as a dentist.

As the Revolutionary War was beginning, the Patriots learned that the British were planning an attack on Concord, Massachusetts. Important Patriot leaders were hiding there, and the Patriots had weapons stored there. Someone needed to warn the men at Concord. Paul Revere was an excellent horseman and a loyal Patriot, but he also had a wife and child. The ride would be very dangerous, but Paul Revere agreed to go.

With his partner William Dawes, Paul Revere made his famous midnight ride, knocking on doors and warning everyone that the British were

---

Describe some ways you might send an emergency message.

_____
_____
_____
_____
_____
_____
_____
_____
_____
_____

coming. The patriots had planned ahead of time that one lantern meant the British were coming by land, and two meant by sea. Paul Revere hung two lanterns in the bell tower in Boston to warn that British troops were arriving by sea.

Along that midnight ride, Paul Revere and William Dawes were stopped by British soldiers. Paul Revere was captured, but William Dawes escaped and continued the ride. The Patriot leaders Sam Adams and John Hancock were warned in time and not captured by the British. The Revolutionary War began. But because of brave colonists like Paul Revere, the 13 colonies won their independence from British rule.

Write a headline that might have been in the Boston newspaper the day after Paul Revere's ride.

_____
_____
_____
_____
_____
_____

Did You Know...

☆ Paul Revere was also a bell maker, engraver, and political cartoonist.

☆ He fixed umbrellas and made eyeglasses.

☆ Young Paul earned money by ringing bells in the church tower.

☆ British soldiers tried to stop his famous ride, but their horses got stuck in a clay pond.

☆ Henry Wadsworth Longfellow wrote a famous poem about Paul Revere's ride.

☆ He had sixteen children.

PAUL REVERE

(sing to the tune of "Three Blind Mice")

1.
Paul Revere
Midnight ride
Warned his men
Go and hide
You'll be attacked
For freedoms sake
You must be brave
And wide-awake
Free from England
Peace at stake
Paul Revere

2.
Old North Church
Steeple high
Candles bright
In the night
One...by land
Two...by sea
Beware the Red Coats,
War will be
Listen now
And you will see
Paul Revere

Rosa Parks

Born 1913

Mother of the
Civil Rights Movement

If you could talk to Rosa Parks, what would you say to her? What questions would you ask her? Write her a letter.

Rosa Parks

Rosa Parks was born in Tuskegee, Alabama in 1913. Her father was a carpenter, and her mother was a teacher.

In the part of the United States in which Rosa Parks grew up, there were laws to keep African-Americans separate from other Americans in many public places. As a young woman, Rosa Parks became a hero to many by standing up to one of these laws. The law stated that African-Americans must sit in a section at the back of town buses. While riding on a bus, Rosa Parks refused to give up her seat to a white man. She was arrested.

In protest, African-Americans in her town refused to use the bus system. Rosa Parks and other African-Americans lost their jobs. Prejudiced people threatened Rosa Parks for standing up for the rights of African-Americans. Rosa Parks and her family were forced to move to Detroit, Michigan.

Her action led more people to protest laws that took away the legal rights of African-Americans. These rights belonging to all

---

Rosa Parks was awarded the Congressional Gold Medal of Honor in 1999. If you could design this medal, what would it look like and what would it say?

American citizens are called Civil Rights. The boycotts, marches, and other protests that eventually restored the rights of African-Americans are together known as the "Civil Rights Movement." The law Rosa Parks stood up to was finally overturned. Everyone could sit on the bus together. Many other racially discriminating laws were overturned, as well.

Since then, Rosa Parks has worked to ensure civil rights for everyone. For her brave action that helped spark a movement, and her tireless work to overturn unfair laws, Rosa Parks is known as the "Mother of the Civil Rights Movement."

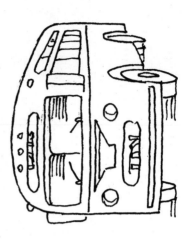

ROSA PARKS

(sing to the tune of "Three Blind Mice")

Rosa Parks
Brave and strong
She worked hard
All day long.

I'll not give up my seat this day!
The front of the bus is where I'll stay!
Fair and equal is the way!
Rosa Parks

Did You Know...

☆ Rosa Parks was a seamstress, like Betsy Ross, who sewed the American flag.

☆ Martin Luther King was her friend.

☆ She loves gospel, hymns, and spiritual music.

☆ She received the Martin Luther King Jr. Nonviolent Peace Prize.

Write about a time you stood up for something you believed in. (Did you defend a friend after someone else called him or her a name, or let another kid join a game when everyone else said no?)

_____
_____
_____
_____
_____
_____
_____

Harriet Tubman

1820–1913

Underground Railroad Conductor

1

List three people that you know that show the same courage and sense of fairness that Harriet Tubman had.

1. _____

2. _____

3. _____

8

Harriet Tubman was born in Bucktown, Maryland in 1826. She was born into an American-American slave family. Her childhood days were full of hard work, and she was not allowed to go to school.

When Harriet Tubman was 25, she married John Tubman. Although she was no longer a slave, Harriet Tubman feared that she would be sold back into slavery. Five years later, Harriet Tubman made her escape to the north along the Underground Railroad. This was not really a railroad, nor was it underground. Underground Railroad was the name for a network of escape routes and safe houses where African-Americans could hide on the way to freedom in the Northern States or Canada. The hiding places were known as "stations" along the Underground Railroad. "Stations" were provided by "station masters." These were white Americans who opposed slavery and wanted to free African-American slaves. The Underground Railroad had to be

---

Stars Away From Slavery

"Passengers" on the Underground Railroad traveled at night, so they often used stars to guide them. Draw lines to match the names with the constellations.

Southern Cross

Orion (hunter)

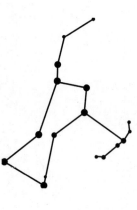

Big Dipper

kept secret as it was illegal to free slaves. Traveling along it was very dangerous. Some "stations" had secret rooms hidden behind closets in houses, or trapdoors in barns.

Harriet Tubman learned more about the working of the Underground Railroad, then risked great danger to help her family members escape. Until slavery was outlawed in the United States, Harriet Tubman spoke out against the practice and worked to end it. During the Civil War, she worked as a nurse and a spy for the Northern States. She also continued to help people to escape and led more than 300 African-Americans to freedom.

After slavery was abolished, Harriet Tubman worked the rest of her long life for the better treatment of women, the elderly, and the poor.

Color this map that shows the Underground Railroad that led slaves from the South to freedom in the North.

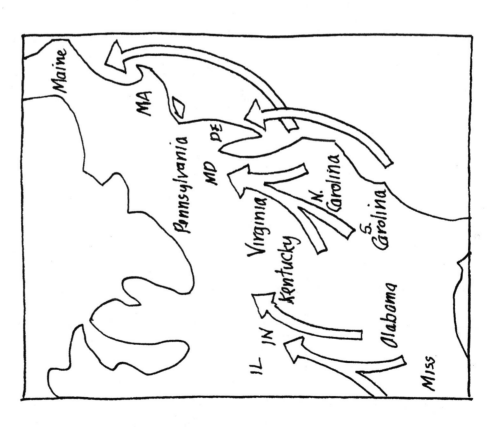

Did You Know...

☆ Harriet Tubman was known as the "Conductor" of the Underground Railroad.

☆ She was also known as "General Tubman."

☆ During the Civil War she served as a nurse.

☆ She also made a good spy. She was valuable to the army because she knew so much about the land.

HARRIET TUBMAN

(sing to the tune of
"I've Been Working on the Railroad")

Tubman worked upon the railroad
During years of war
She helped to free
The many people
Who slaved and
Did the chores

She said, underground you'll be safe.
Soon you will be free
I will help you to discover
A land of liberty

Go Harriet
Go Harriet
Tubman was her name
Go Harriet
Go Harriet
Freedom is your fame

Susan B. Anthony
1820–1906

Fighter for Women's Rights

List five qualities of a leader.

1. _____
2. _____
3. _____
4. _____
5. _____

Susan B. Anthony

was born in Adams, Massachusetts in 1820. Her family were Quakers with a long tradition of being activists, and were part of the anti-slavery movement. Susan B. Anthony was schooled at home, and at an early age developed a sense of justice.

She became an educated and independent young woman, and was outspoken about difficult issues facing women at the time. Women were not allowed to vote back then, and Susan B. Anthony was arrested with other women for trying to cast votes in a public election. She and these others were suffragists. A suffragist is a person who wants more people to have the right to vote.

DEMOCRACY IN ACTION

Now vote on the same issue, but this time, anyone with an R in their first name is not allowed to vote.

FOR	AGAINST

How was the result different?

_____

_____

_____

Why was the second vote unfair?

_____

_____

_____

Susan B. Anthony continued to speak out about equal rights for women and against slavery. She persuaded colleges to admit women as students, and traveled all over the country trying to get laws passed to allow women to vote.

In 1920, the Nineteenth Amendment was added to the U. S. Constitution, allowing all American adult women to vote. Also known as the Susan B. Anthony Amendment, this right to vote is due to Susan B. Anthony, the suffragists, and many others who fought for equal rights.

DEMOCRACY IN ACTION

As a class, choose an issue that must be decided upon. Take a vote.

Issue:

FOR	AGAINST

Susan B. Anthony had a dollar coin made for her. Color this coin.

SUSAN B. ANTHONY
(sing to the tune of "This Old Man")

Susan B.
Anthony

Fought for women's rights
You see

Right to vote
And right to take a stand

We all count
In this great land

Abraham Lincoln

1809–1865

"Four score and seven years ago…"

Abraham Lincoln was known to be kind. Make a list of acts of kindness you have performed recently:

Abraham Lincoln was born on a farm in Kentucky in 1809. The farm work was hard, his family was poor, and his mother died when he was just nine years old. But Abraham Lincoln grew tall and strong, and spend his free time reading, reading and reading!

Abraham Lincoln studied hard, and grew up to be a lawyer. He then became a Congressman, and in 1861 was elected President of the United States. He was President at a very difficult time for this country. Americans disagreed so strongly about slavery that they went to war with one another. Most people in the northern states thought African-Americans should be free. In the southern states, many people needed workers on their large plantations and did not want to pay them. Many Americans died fighting the Civil War.

With the Emancipation Proclamation, Abraham Lincoln announced that all Americans were free and equal under the law

ABRAHAM LINCOLN
(sing to the tune of "Yankee Doodle")

There was a man named Abraham
Lincoln, Honest Abe
He set about to free the slaves
In war between the states.

Abraham, born brave and strong
His portrait's on a penny
16th President was he
beloved by so many

and that all slaves must be freed. Still, not all slave-owners freed their slaves. Many slaves were not told they had been made free by United States law until after the end of the Civil War.

The famous speech that Abraham Lincoln made to honor those who died in the Civil War is known as the Gettysburg Address.

Abraham Lincoln was shot while attending a play at Ford's Theatre in Washington, D.C. He was the sixteenth American President, and the first to be assassinated.

Did You Know...

☆ Lincoln was born in a log cabin.

☆ Lincoln grew to be 6 feet 4 inches tall.

☆ Lincoln's portrait is on the penny and the five-dollar bill.

☆ The Lincoln Memorial in Washington, D.C. honors President Lincoln.

☆ Lincoln was known for his tall black stovepipe hat.

Describe how your house is different from the log cabin that Lincoln lived in.

_____
_____
_____
_____
_____
_____
_____
_____

Color the Lincoln Memorial in Washington, DC.

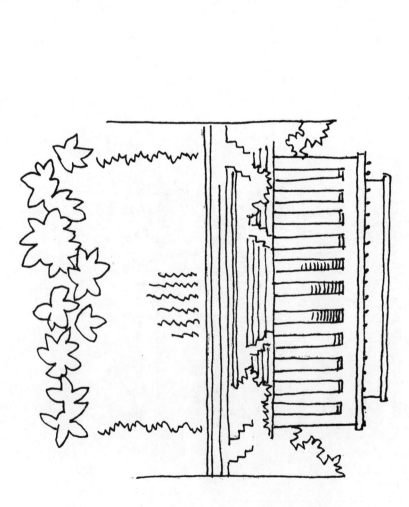

George Washington Carver

1864–1963

Plant Scientist

1

MAKE YOUR OWN PEANUT BUTTER!

Peanut Butter

Use a blender with adult help.

Put 1 cup of salted peanuts into the blender.

Add 1 tablespoon of oil.

Blend till smooth.

Spread it on bread!

8

George Washington Carver

was born in 1860 in Diamond Grove, Missouri into a family kept in slavery. During the Civil War, he and his mother were kidnapped by people who hoped to sell them for a profit. While with the kidnappers, he became very sick with whooping cough.

The white slave-owners who owned George Washington Carver searched for him for a long time. In the end, they traded a horse to get him back. Since he was a sick child, he did not work as much as the others in the fields. He wandered through the woods learning about plants and flowers, and taught himself how to read and write. His first school was a one-room schoolhouse

When he was older, he applied to a university, but was rejected because he was black. Instead, he went to Simpson College in Iowa, and graduated from Iowa State University. He had always been interested in nature, and studied to be a plant scientist.

Write the directions for making a peanut butter sandwich. What do you do first, second, and third?

1. _____

2. _____

3. _____

George Washington Carver went on to teach at an African-American college called the Tuskegee Institute. He developed the practice of crop rotation, which is planting one crop (like peanuts) one year, and a different crop (like cotton) on the same land the next year. Different crops use different parts of the soil, so by changing them every year, the soil remains more rich in nutrients.

Since he had encouraged farmers to grow peanuts, George Washington Carver wanted to think of uses for peanuts to make the crop more valuable. He came up with over 300 ways to use peanuts. He also found many uses for sweet potatoes.

George Washington Carver became a scientist at a time when it was rare for African-Americans to get a college education. This brave man made important contributions to science and helped blaze a trail for African-Americans seeking a better life.

Did You Know...

☆ George Washington Carver was the nation's first well-known African American scientist.

☆ His birthplace is a national monument.

☆ He learned from a young age that white people and black people were treated differently.

GEORGE WASHINGTON CARVER

(sing to the tune of "On Top of Old Smokey")

George Washington Carver
loved plants strong and tall.
He showed us that peanuts
are useful to all.

Rotate them with cotton
each year that's for sure.
You'll grow tasty peanuts.
Your land gives you more.

He worked with potatoes
So orange and sweet
he told all the farmers
"They're so sweet to eat!"

It's all about nature
Work hard, study too
like scientist Carver
It's the smart thing to do.

PEANUTS, PEANUTS!

Check off the ways you like to eat peanuts.

☐ plain peanuts

☐ peanut butter

☐ peanut brittle

☐ peanut butter cups

☐ peanuts and raisins together

☐ I do not eat peanuts.

Martin Luther King, Jr.

1929–1968

Civil Rights Leader

Martin Luther King, Jr.

Martin Luther King, Jr. was a great man who worked for racial equality in the United States of America. He was born on January 15, 1929, in Atlanta, Georgia. He grew up to become one of the most influential and unforgettable people of the century.

Both his father and grandfather were ministers. His mother was a schoolteacher who taught him how to read before he went to school. When he went to school, he became an excellent student.

He graduated from Morehouse College, then he became a minister and moved to Alabama. He married Coretta Scott in 1953. In the 1950's, Dr. King became active in the movement for civil rights and racial equality.

Do you have a dream you'd like to share with others? Write a speech describing a vision you have for the future.

_____
_____
_____
_____
_____
_____
_____
_____
_____
_____

He led the civil rights movement in the 1950's and 60's, and fought for equal rights among all races.

He organized the Montgomery Bus Boycott, fought against discrimination in voting registration, and led nonviolent marches and movements all over the United States. One of his famous speeches, known as the "I Have a Dream" speech, was delivered to over 250,000 people in Washington DC in 1963.

He organized many other peaceful demonstrations that protested the unfair treatment of African-Americans. He won the Nobel Peace Prize in 1964.

Dr. King was assassinated on April 4, 1968, in Memphis, Tennessee. We observe his birthday as a special holiday every year, on the third Monday in January.

I HAVE A DREAM

Here are the most famous words from Martin Luther King's most famous speech. What do you think he meant? Put this idea into your own words.

I have a dream my four little children will one day live in a nation where they will not be judged by the color of their skin but by the content of their character. I have a dream today!

_____
_____
_____
_____
_____
_____

MARTIN LUTHER KING

(sing to the tune of "If You're Happy and You Know It")

Black and white,
Fair and equal,
One and all.

Black and white,
Fair and equal,
One and all.

Martin Luther King reminds us
That equality should guide us

Black and white,
Fair and equal,
One and all.

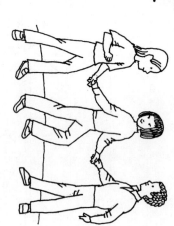

What are some ways you treat your friends and family fairly?

_____
_____
_____
_____
_____
_____

Equal Rights for All People

George Washington

1732–1799

Father of Our Country

1

Would you have liked George Washington's job of being the first president? Why or why not?

_____
_____
_____
_____
_____
_____
_____
_____

8

Read, Sing, and Learn Mini-Books: Famous Americans Scholastic Professional Books

George Washington

George Washington was born in Westmoreland County, Virginia in 1732. He spent his childhood at Ferry Farm, Virginia, a small home on the banks of the Rappahanock River. When he was sixteen, George Washington became a surveyor. He rode through areas that were not yet settled, measuring and mapping the land. He did so much riding as a surveyor that he became a very good horseman. He was interested in horse racing and knew the famous racehorses of the time.

In 1759, he married Martha Custis. George and Martha Washington lived on a beautiful plantation home on the Potomac River in Mount Vernon, Virginia.

During the Revolutionary War, George Washington was a General and led the American Colonies in their fight for freedom from England. He was well-loved for helping the soldiers work together, and for leading the Colonies to victory. After the war, George Washington looked forward to returning home to his plantation.

The Colonies were now states in a new country: the United States of America. But the American states were not used to working together to support each other and the country. The new country needed a strong leader to bring

Compare George Washington with the president today.

Washington _____

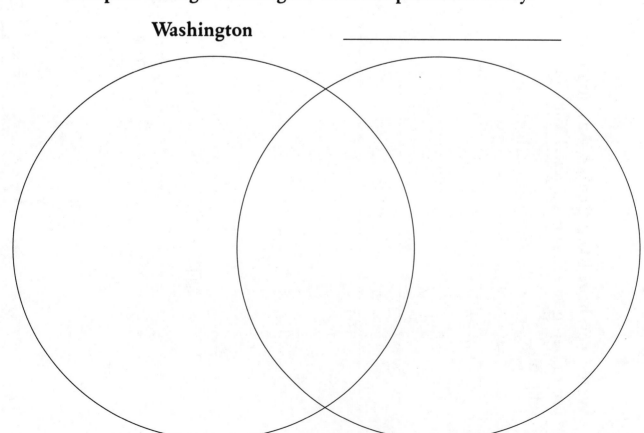

everyone together. People immediately thought of George Washington, and some wanted him to become king. Even though it would mean not returning home to the plantation, George Washington was willing to lead the country. He did not want the new country to be led by a king. He felt the country should have a leader elected by the people. He worked with other founders of the country to develop a democracy, the form of government in the United States that is still used today.

In the first Presidential election, every state elected George Washington the first President of the United States. George Washington was a strong leader who brought Americans together in their new country. For his roles in leading the Colonies to victory, helping to organize the first government, and being the first President of the United States, George Washington is respected as the "Father of Our Country."

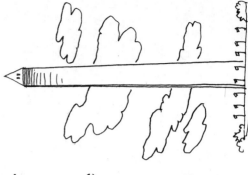

3

Did You Know...

☆ Washington loved being a farmer. He had many other jobs throughout his life: surveyor, general and president!

☆ His portrait is on both the dollar bill and the quarter.

☆ The Washington Monument in Washington, D.C. was built in his honor.

☆ Both Washington, DC and Washington state are named for him.

☆ He wore a wig, which was considered fashionable at the time.

6

GEORGE WASHINGTON

(sing to the tune of "Yankee Doodle")

There was a man named Washington
Virginia-born and bred
He grew to be first president,
"He's great!" is what they said.

Farmer, leader, president,
Mt. Vernon was his place,
Born at Pope's Creek, Ferry Farm
A dollar bill, his face

George Washington's portrait is on the dollar bill.
Draw yourself on a dollar bill!

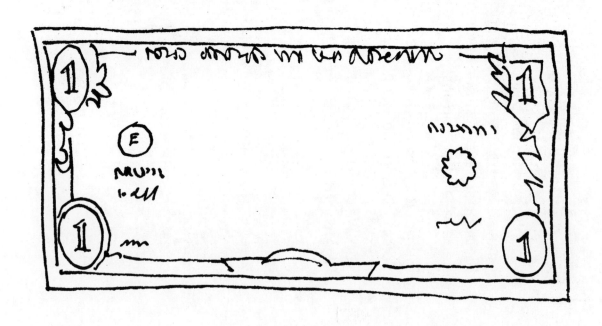